MW01181637

HANDLING MALICIOUS
ANIMAL MAGNETISM

HANDLING MALICIOUS ANIMAL MAGNETISM

A Collection of Timeless Articles
on Detecting and Overcoming
Evil through Prayer in
Christian Science

The Bookmark
Santa Clarita, California

Library of Congress Control Number: 2003105831

ISBN 0-930227-55-7
Handling malicious animal magnetism: a collection of timeless
articles on detecting and overcoming evil through prayer in
Christian Science / [by Mary Baker Eddy ... [et al.]]. p. cm.
CONTENTS: Introduction -- The chief delusion -Malicious
animal magnetism -Ways that are vain and Application of ways
that are vain -Demonology -Animla magnetism -- Forms of
animal magnetism defined -Wiser than serpents -- The impersonal nature of evil -Handling animal magnetism -- Recognizing
one's enemy -Mental malpractice -- Mora idiocy -- Radiation
and absorption.

1. Christian Science--Doctrines. 2. Good and evil. 3.
Prayer--Christianity. I. Eddy, Mary Baker, 1821-1910.

BX6913.H36 2003
289.5
QB103-700151

Published by
The Bookmark
Post Office Box 801143
Santa Clarita, California 91380

CONTENTS

INTRODUCTION

There has developed over the last century the belief that good and evil are relative, that there is no absolute Truth. With the loss of the strong moral foundation that Christianity gave the world, evil has become so aggressive as to threaten the safety and well being of all humanity. With secret hypnosis, witchcraft, subliminal suggestion, and other forms of mind control becoming more sophisticated, subtle, and hidden in their operation, it would seem another Dark Age is gathering. With this growing practice of mind control the undefended mind seems to have no means of escaping the many forms of malicious animal magnetism abroad today.

One answer to this growing threat of mind control is found in the Scriptures where good and evil are *not* relative, but clearly defined as right and wrong. It is said of Christ Jesus that he loved God and hated iniquity, calling evil a liar and the father of it. He came to show us how to overcome disease, insanity, adversity, lack — even death itself — through obedience to God's laws. He taught others how to overcome the seeming power of evil, so that his followers could heal as he did.

For three centuries after his ascension, spiritual healing did take place among the early Christians; but as time dimmed the inspiration and enlightenment that Jesus gave the world, the healing works of these faithful followers gradually disappeared.

With the discovery of Christian Science in 1866 the world was given the scientific laws underlying Jesus' healing works. It was again possible for humanity to practice spiritual healing and have a refuge from all forms of evil, including malicious mental malpractice.

The fundamental truth underlying this healing power is the fact that God, good, alone is real, and evil is powerless and unreal — an illusion, a form of hypnotism that can be overcome through prayer.

This is not a theory, but a proven fact evidenced by the thousands of healings that are on record, going back to the time when Christian Science was first discovered. The healing works of early Christianity are again taking place by those who understand that God is All-in-all, and evil has no power or reality.

To claim evil to be unreal seems against all reason, but those who accept this idea on faith and learn to challenge evil as hypnotic suggestion in their own consciousness find that such prayer heals them and protects them against mental malpractice.

The world has believed in the reality of evil since time began, so that reversing this belief and understanding evil as hypnosis requires a dedicated study of Christian Science. As the full scope of its teaching unfolds, the student finds he can indeed heal as Christ Jesus healed, and he can protect himself against the harmful influence of animal magnetism.

This book has been compiled to help you undertake the task of being free of the illusion of animal magnetism. It includes some of the best known works on this subject. Mary Baker Eddy penned many powerful statements exposing evil's unreality and the need to understand how it claims to operate. This collection opens with four of her strongest works on animal magnetism, including an excerpt from the chapter on "Demonology" from the third edition of the Christian Science textbook, *Science and Health with Key to the Scriptures*. These statements, first published in the late 1800s, were too advanced for the Victorian Age. She found that students new to Christian Science were either frightened by such ideas, or they perverted them and began using malicious malpractice against her and her students. She soon realized that she could not continue to teach openly on this subject. But there were those loyal students who understood what she privately taught them on this, and their writings are also included in this collection. These writings provide a powerful statement on the need to handle malicious animal magnetism and how to do it.

Aside from the teachings of Christian Science, the average person has little or no means for protecting his mind from the threat of mental attack and invasion. But the scientific form of prayer found in this Science provides such protection. When we acknowledge the allness of God and reject the power and reality of evil, this prayer heals because it is based on more than faith in the power of good over evil. The logic underlying this fundamental truth is explained in Mrs. Eddy's profound book, *Unity of Good*. In it she writes, "As God is Mind, if this Mind is familiar with evil, all cannot be good therein. Our infinite model would be taken away. What is in eternal Mind must be reflected in man, Mind's image. How then could man escape, or hope to escape, from a knowledge which is everlasting in his creator?" She also tells us, " . . . an acknowledgement of the perfection of the infinite Unseen confers a healing power nothing else can. An uncontestable point in divine Science is, that because God is All, a realization of this fact dispels even a sense or consciousness of sin, and brings us nearer to God, bringing out the highest phenomona of the All-Mind."

Spiritual healing requires more than faith in God's goodness. We need to understand what evil claims to be, how it operates, how to detect it, and protect our mind against its influence.

The ideas presented in this book are challenging, thought provoking, and extremely effective in learning the art of spiritual healing and mental self-defense. Although they may seem somewhat overwhelming when you first read them, you will find in time that they become a staff to lean on and a weapon for disarming the influence of evil's suggestions. You find you can heal with confidence when you know how to handle malicious animal magnetism.

A. B.

THE CHIEF DELUSION

(From the First Edition of *Retrospection and Introspection.*)

by

Mary Baker Eddy

For all error there is but one statement: namely, that error is a false belief and the generic term for belief is Animal Magnetism. All forms of this belief are illusion, a false sense of life, substance, and intelligence as existing in and of matter, opposed to spiritual Life, Truth, and Love. This delusion must be met in all its subtleties, — in its so-called pleasures and pains of sense, passion, appetite, lust, pride, hatred, envy, malice.

Phenomenally, all error is Animal Magnetism. Webster defines Animal Magnetism to be "a supposed agency of a peculiar and mysterious nature, said to have a powerful influence on the patient, when acted upon by, or brought into contact with, the will of the operator." This definition applies also to Mesmerism. In common usage the term Mesmerism, or Hypnotism, falls short of its entire meaning, which should include those phenomena of Animal Magnetism by which the victim is affected involuntarily and without contact or consent.

This incomplete definition fails also to define self-magnetism, by which animal life is said to be carried on, and by which brain and nerves communicate through a vital fluid.

I have seen a person, when under the effect of Hypnotism, obey the will of one who was neither present, nor known to be attempting any such influence over him. I doubted whether this effect could be produced without the consent of the person to be affected; but this doubt was removed when I witnessed with horror, a superinduced state of involuntary mesmerism.

The methods of Animal Magnetism, especially its secret work, should be exposed. This alone can protect the people from a future Reign of Terror, far surpassing the error and terrorism of the Dark Ages. One has nothing to fear from this evil, if he is conscious of its claims and its presence, and, on the basis of Christian Science, understands its impotence. Animal Magnetism is the opposite of Christian Science; and its effect on the senses is readily removed by the latter, if the cause of this effect is understood.

Ambitious students — who by a mental and audible transmission of their own thoughts influence the lives of other students — have only succeeded in staying their own usefulness, obscuring their own light and the light that had dawned on those who follow them. Such erratic movements have made many factions, but never yet have accomplished their purposes, nor benefited one human being.

Doubters of the existence or the evil of mental malpractice, sneerers at the probability of its methods, will at no distant day have their eyes sharply opened. I have been too charitable towards this evil, through sheer ignorance. He who is guilty of mental malpractice scoffs at its possibilities. He who bears witness to them is the friend of humanity.

Let us follow the example of Jesus, the Master Metaphysician, and gain sufficient knowledge of error to destroy it with Truth. Evil is not mastered by evil; it can only be overcome with Good. This brings out the nothingness of evil; and the eternal somethingness of God, vindicates Principle, and improves our present personality. We must accept the responsibility of acting rightly and uncovering iniquity.

The loyal Christian Scientist is incapable alike of abusing the practice of Mind-healing, or of healing on a material basis. Animal Magnetism has no basis. It is illusion. It is mortal mind, while Mind is immortal. It stands for whatever is destructive to health and morals. Our Master was led to Calvary's cross by evil influences, and it is the function of Christian Science to uncover and cast out kindred evils.

If an honest Christian Scientist can be deceived into believing that only chance is at work, instead of malicious mental influence, he must rid himself of this delusion before he can heal; for it is a Delilah who would lead him into the toils of the enemy, where Cerberus (the apt symbol of Animal Magnetism) waits to devour the self-deceived.

The silent arguments of those who themselves turn away, are designed to turn away others, from the Spirit of Christian Science. The work of healing, in the Science of Mind, is the most sacred and salutary power which can be wielded. My Christian students, impressed with the true sense of the great work before them, enter this strait and narrow path and work conscientiously.

This century, blessed with the advent of Christian Science, is also subject, as others have been, to false teachers and healers, who claim to understand and demonstrate that of which they apprehend but a fraction, — who multiply words without knowledge, and know just enough to render their error and ignorance more plausible, but not less dangerous.

Unscientific theory and wrong mental practice are more fatal to sanitary reform, sound morals, health and longevity, than is the old-fashioned empirical treatment, by blood-letting, poisonous drugs, and the other multifarious modes of frightening people to death. The name Mind Cure is sometimes conferred upon Hypnotism and Animal Magnetism; but these methods are the antipodes of Science.

What is termed mortal and material power, as manifest life, is graphically defined by Caldron, the famous Spanish poet, who wrote:

What is life? Tis but a madness.
What is life? A mere illusion,
Fleeting pleasure, fond delusion,
Short-lived joy, that ends in sadness,
Whose most constant substance seems,
But the dream of other dreams.

MALICIOUS ANIMAL MAGNETISM

(From *The Christian Science Journal* of 1889)

by

Mary Baker Eddy

One of the greatest crimes practiced in, or known to the ages, is mental assassination. A mind liberated from the beliefs of sense, to do good, by perverting its power becomes warped into the lines of evil without let or hindrance. A mind taught its power to touch other minds by the transference of thought, for the ends of restoration from sickness, or — grandest of all — the reformation and almost transformation, into the living image and likeness of God — this mind by misusing its freedom reaches the degree of total moral depravity.

Does the community know this criminal? He sits at the friendly board and fireside; he goes to their places of worship; he takes his victim by the hand, and all the time claims the power and carries the will to stab to the heart, to take character and life from this friend who gives him his hand in full trust, and has perhaps toiled and suffered to benefit and bless him.

What are some of the methods of this evil, this satan let loose? What are some of the means through which these mental assassins effect their purposes? To alienate friends, to divide households, to make people sick and sinners; these are their common instrumentalities.

Their methods of operation are to infuse silently into the thoughts of those they wish to use as instruments, a false sense of the individual selected as their victim. Long acquaintance, tried fidelity, experiences that have knit hearts together, all become as nothing before these endeavors. The mind of the individual on whom they thus operate is filled with hatred of the dearest friend, is made incapable of a just judgment of this friend. Prior knowledge of him seems to be obscured, put out, annihilated, and a new image of thought to be created — one idea of individual character to be lost and another one formed in the mind of him whom they would cause to hate his friend.

In this dilemma of thought, they get the audible falsehood into his mind, tell him how his friend has slandered him, is trying to injure him. If he is a Scientist, they then say to him, "'Mr. Smith', or 'Mrs. Jones' is preventing your success in healing patients, or is making your family sick, and the only way you can meet this is to take the case up, and to treat your patients against Mrs. Jones' mental malpractice; if you can destroy your patients' fear of Mrs. Jones, or can choke her off by any means however foul, you are conscientiously bound to do it, and of two evils this is choosing the least." There may be a hundred or more operators all set at work at this very job, to kill Mrs. Jones, or to save their patients or themselves, according as the directing malevolence may dictate. The said Jones is all the while as unconscious of this conspiracy as the unborn babe. The mental assassins are morally responsible for the consequences, and God alone can save her life from the fatal effects of this malice aforethought of the first party, and the culpable blindness of the second, whom they have misguided.

When the work of the mental assassin culminates, and the victim falls, the doctors are consulted and call it heart disease or some other 'visitation of God,' and thus they try to carry the age along on their deceptions.

This criminal practice, this 'wickedness in high places,' has accumulated in subtilty of method until it culminates at this period in 'spiritual wickedness' and poses its power to do evil against the spiritual power in Christian Science to demonstrate good. When first denounced by me 'from the housetops,' in *Science and Health* thirteen years ago, the revelation was received with incredulity, with derision, with pity. Today Scientists are learning, and the general public is experiencing more and more, the terrible realities of mental malpractice and assassination.

It is no longer possible to keep still concerning these things — nay, it is criminal to hold silence and to cover crime that grows bolder and picks off its victims as sharpshooters pick off the officers of an attacking force.

These secret, heaven-defying enormities must be proclaimed, or we become guilty before God as accessory after the fact. If a friend were fallen upon and maltreated or murdered before our eyes, should we hold ourselves guiltless — should we count ourselves men and women — if we buried the secret of the violence and our knowledge of the assassins?

Are we such cowards, knowing the facts that we do know, as to turn and run? Shall we see the evil, the deadly danger that threatens our brother and hide ourselves, flee away not warning him?

The Science of Mind uncovers to Scientists secret sin, even more distinctly than so-called physical crimes are visible to the personal senses; crime is always veiled in obscurity; but Science fastens guilt upon its author through mind, with the certainty and directness of the eye of God Himself.

Human laws will eventually be framed for these criminals that now go unwhipped of human justice. Human law even now recognizes crime as mental, for it seeks always the motive; rude counterfeit as it is of Divine Justice, it metes out punishment or pardons, according as it finds or finds not the evil intent, the mental element. The time has come for instructing human justice so that these secret criminals shall tremble before the omnipotent finger that points them out to the human executioner.

This is not an invitation to promiscuous denunciation. The time is not ripe for that, but God tells us now to uncover this wickedness, to expose its methods, to accumulate the evidence of its enormities. The human mind must be instructed by facts, taught how to recognize the signs of these secret crimes as they are worked on individuals, and also the method of self-protection, the antidotes found only in Divine Science.

God has bidden me to uncover this wickedness, and I follow His voice. Let all Scientists aid in this work, first, by bringing out in their reports on the practice of healing, careful statements of the facts of malicious animal magnetism that are daily passing before their eyes. I am not inviting them to indiscriminating condemnation, but to bring out such facts as have come within their own field of observation.

I have put on paper enough to reveal criminal magnetism, and to meet its developments for time to come, when my voice will be no longer heard. But God does not let us wait. He tells us to denounce now some of the crimes of malicious mind, and to teach as fully as the age can bear and as the developments of this crime demand, its methods and their unfailing antidote.

I will now answer some questions that correspondents have asked me, concerning my teaching of and ways of dealing with malicious animal magnetism.

One correspondent asks, "Do I teach the same with regard to mesmerism to all my students?"

My answer is, I do, in substance the same; the manner of expressing my thoughts may vary, but never the idea. Every student who has been through my class understands fully how to handle the ignorant animal magnetism, termed sickness, and I have taught, as fully as God has allowed, how to deal with the malicious element. He tells me how to meet its growing wickedness by fuller revelations.

"Do I approve of treating personally for malicious mesmerism the offending malpractitioner, even when the malpractitioner is attempting to kill some one, and Scientists know it? Shall they treat the offender personally?"

I answer, if they do treat thus, they prolong their own under-taking. The altitude of Christian Science is Omnipotence. Truth is given us for this purpose — to destroy error and make man free in the impersonal Christ.

"Do I employ students to do the work I have not the time to do?" in other words, in trying to injure fellow beings.

I would commit suicide sooner than do that; I have laid upon the altar too much for my fellow mortals, to undo my life work, and now turn to injure them. The very misguided ones, the deluded ones who would constrain others to believe this for my hurt, know better. These deceivers are under a demoni-cal spell. May God open their eyes and save them from future condemnation.

WAYS THAT ARE VAIN

(From *The First Church of Christ, Scientist and Miscellany*)

by

Mary Baker Eddy

Certain individuals entertain the notion that Christian Science Mind-healing should be two-sided, and only denounce error in general — saying nothing, in particular, of error that is damning men. They are sticklers for a false, convenient peace, straining at gnats and swallowing camels. The unseen wrong to individuals and society they are too cowardly, too ignorant, or too wicked to uncover, and excuse themselves by denying that this evil exists. This mistaken way, of hiding sin in order to maintain harmony, has licensed evil, allowing it first to smoulder, and then break out in devouring flames. All that error asks is to be let alone; even as in Jesus' time the unclean spirits cried out, "Let us alone; what have we to do with thee?"

Animal magnetism, in its ascending steps of evil, entices its victim by unseen, silent arguments. Reversing the modes of good, in their silent allurements to health and holiness, it impels mortal mind into error of thought, and tempts into the committal of acts foreign to the natural inclinations. The victims lose their individuality, and lend themselves as willing tools to carry out the designs of their worst enemies, even those who would induce their self-destruction. Animal magnetism fosters suspicious distrust where honor is due, fear where courage should be strongest, reliance where there should be avoidance, a belief in safety where there is most danger; and these miserable lies, poured constantly into his mind, fret and confuse it, spoiling that individual's disposition, undermining his health, and sealing his doom, unless the cause of the mischief is found out and destroyed.

Other minds are made dormant by it, and the victim is in a state of semi-individuality, with a mental haziness which admits of no intellectual culture or spiritual growth. The state induced by this secret evil influence is a species of intoxication, in which the victim is led to believe and do what he would never, otherwise, think or do voluntarily.

This intricate method of animal magnetism is the essence, or spirit, of evil, which makes mankind drunken. In this era it is taking the place of older and more open sins, and other forms of intoxication. A harder fight will be necessary to expose the cause and effects of this evil influence, than has been required to put down the evil effects of alcohol. The alcoholic habit is the use of higher forms of matter, wherewith to do evil; whereas animal magnetism is the highest form of mental evil, wherewith to complete the sum total of sin.

The question is often asked, Why is there so much dissension among mental practitioners? We answer, Because they do not practise in strict accordance with the teaching of Christian Science Mind-healing. If they did, there would be unity of action. Being like the disciples of old, "with one accord in one place," they would receive a spiritual influx impossible under other conditions, and so would recognize and resist the animal magnetism by which they are being deceived and misled.

The mental malpractitioner, interfering with the rights of Mind, destroys the true sense of Science, and loses his own power to heal. He tries to compensate himself for his own loss by hindering in every way conceivable the success of others. You will find this practitioner saying that animal magnetism never troubles him, but that Mrs. Eddy teaches animal magnetism; and he says this to cover his crime of mental malpractice, in furtherance of unscrupulous designs.

11

The natural fruits of Christian Science Mind-healing are harmony, brotherly love, spiritual growth and activity. The malicious aim of perverted mind-power, or animal magnetism, is to paralyze good and give activity to evil. It starts factions and engenders envy and hatred, but as activity is by no means a right of evil and its emissaries, they ought not to be encouraged in it. Because this age is cursed with one rancorous and lurking foe to human weal, those who are the truest friends of mankind, and conscientious in their desire to do right and to live pure and Christian lives, should be more zealous to do good, more watchful and vigilant. Then they will be proportionately successful and bring out glorious results.

Unless one's eyes are opened to the modes of mental malpractice, working so subtly that we mistake its suggestions for the impulses of our own thought, the victim will allow himself to drift in the wrong direction without knowing it. Be ever on guard against this enemy. Watch your thoughts, and see whether they lead you to God and into harmony with His true followers. Guard and strengthen your own citadel more strongly. Thus you will grow wiser and better through every attack of your foe, and the Golden Rule will not rust for lack of use or be misinterpreted by the adverse influence of animal magnetism.

APPLICATION OF *WAYS THAT ARE VAIN*
This statement was given by Mrs. Eddy to John Winthrop after she wrote "Ways that Are Vain," found in *Miscellany*.

Animal magnetism in its ascending steps of evil cannot entice me with unseen silent arguments. It cannot reverse the modes of good in their silent allurements to health and holiness. Animal magnetism cannot impel me into error of thought or tempt me into a committal of acts foreign to my natural inclination. I cannot become a victim of animal magnetism and thereby lose my individuality.

Animal magnetism cannot cause me to lend myself as a willing tool to carry out the designs of my worst enemies. Animal magnetism cannot foster in me suspicious distrust where honor is due, fear where courage should be strongest, reliance where there should be avoidance, or a belief in safety where there is the greatest danger. These miserable lies cannot be poured into my mind to fret and confuse me.

Animal magnetism cannot spoil my disposition, and undermine my health or seal my doom. The cause of the mischief, Truth will uncover and destroy. I cannot be made dormant by animal magnetism nor can it induce me into a state of semi-individuality. I cannot become mentally lazy nor be led into a state that admits of no intellectual culture or spiritual growth.

Animal magnetism cannot induce me to believe or to do what I would not otherwise think or do voluntarily. I cannot become drunken with the intoxication of the senses. There is no power in mental evil. I desire to practice in strict accord with the teachings of Christian Science Mind-healing, therefore I cannot express or feel any belief that mental evil has power. I can and will express unity of action with the people of God, good, being as the disciples of old "of one accord in one place." I and all who love Christian Science can receive spiritual influx.

Animal magnetism, you cannot separate me from God; you cannot dim my spiritual perception. You cannot make a law that I cannot heal myself or others. God is my strength and my refuge, the only intelligence. Animal magnetism, you are not Mind, nor any of its attributes. You are not power, nor intelligence. You are not existence, but a nonentity. You cannot produce any belief of poison, arsenic or any other kind, for there is no poison, and if there were, it could not touch or harm me, for we are told we can handle serpents and if we drink any deadly thing it shall not harm us.

Animal magnetism, you cannot produce any beliefs in me nor bring back an old belief; for there is no belief or believer, nor can you bring any belief into my family or patients, friends or coworkers. "For I am persuaded that neither death nor life, nor angels nor principalities, nor powers, nor things present, nor things to come, nor height, nor depth, nor any other creature shall be able to separate me from the Love of God which is in Christ Jesus our Lord." (Rom. 8:3)

Animal magnetism cannot think, do, nor feel. It has no existence nor creation; never has been, is not, nor ever shall be, and cannot manifest itself in grades of error, electricity, mediumship, theosophy, agnosticism, psychology, astrology, soothsaying, hypnotism, R.C., or any other form of sickness, sin or death, for God is All-in-all, the only creator of the only universe, and we are all His children, and realize the omnipresence of God.

I can recognize and resist animal magnetism. I cannot be deceived nor misled. Animal magnetism, and mental malpractice cannot interfere with the rights of Mind nor destroy the true sense of Science. Animal magnetism cannot hinder in any possible way the success I am honestly striving for. I can only express the natural results of Christian Science Mind-healing which are harmony, brotherly love, spiritual growth and activity.

Animal magnetism cannot paralyze good nor give activity to evil. My eyes are open to the modes of malicious animal magnetism. I cannot mistake its suggestions for the impulse of my thoughts. I cannot drift in the wrong direction. Through the power of God, I can ever be on guard against this tendency.

The student is not where he can heal without argument. Animal magnetism is at work to deprive loyal students of their power and mentally persuade them not to argue. *Why?* Because this Truth-telling is a great neutralizer of error's lies. Keep up your mental arguments and tell others to do so. Be watchful and every day ask Love to keep you from temptation and give you daily bread, grace to know and do God's work. Try to realize the omnipresence of Life and Love, and with the inbreathing of His presence, arouse

14

yourself to a clear sense of God's power, the eternal ever-conscious Mind which knows only Life. Fear and death are powerless in even a faint perception of these declarations of Truth. Animal magnetism, ignorant or malicious, you cannot deprive me of intelligence, Truth and Love.

O Love, just take me in, give me one Mind, one consciousness, and make me love my neighbor as myself. All is love and peace and joy. Heaven is right here. Love reigns. There is no strife. "Peace be still." Truth has destroyed all error. Love has destroyed all hate. All is Love, peace and harmony. You must know that animal magnetism cannot gain nor assist power or action through any mortal or mortals, and if you know it, it cannot touch you. The words you will need are, "It is I, be not afraid." "Because He has set His love upon me, therefore will I deliver him." There never was a moment when evil was real. There are no mortals who can reflect evil upon the earth, and you must disarm the claim of personality to make room for the dear love that destroys malpractice. There is no mortal you that can be touched by wickedness or malicious words. If God is All- in-all, you need not be afraid. Anything you can be afraid of is not real. It is unreal, useless, senseless. Abide in the 91st Psalm and in the 23rd. Read page 578 of *Science and Health,* and know that such abiding is treatment and protection. There is nothing outside divine Mind that can make laws or influence you. If you could but see the sublimity of your hope, the infinite capacity of your being, the grandeur of your outlook, you would let error kill itself. It has come to you for life and you give it all the life it has. You prolong its life by giving it a temporary sense of existence.

DEMONOLOGY

(Excerpt from the Chapter on "Demonology"
from *Science and Health,* Third Edition)

by

Mary Baker Eddy

Mortal mind affects the body to good or bad results, and
has found a way of reaching other minds, and governing the body,
unknown to the individual, as directly and with more certainty, than
the mesmerist who comes honestly before the footlights with his
performance.

If one decent deed is done by the mental malpractitioner,
ten that are terrible are also done; and if one disease is allayed by
this mental outlaw, another one, more dangerous is induced. Mesmerism is practiced both with and without manipulation; but the evil
deed without a sign is also done by the manipulator and mental
malpractitioner.

Without doubt there are honest individuals practising mesmerism, not knowing their method is unsafe. But those are not the
dangerous doctors of whom we speak. It is the malicious mesmerist, the mental malpractitioner, to whom we refer, that avails himself of a secret method on every occasion, or on any, to influence
the mind in the direction that envy, vanity, avarice, sensuality, or
revenge dictates. We have little faith in a mental practitioner who
does not come under the most solemn restraint in his practice. The
real metaphysician alone is safe from the encroachment of this
mental power, released to do good, when it is turned to the opposite
practice of mesmerism. The exhibitor of this barefaced insolence
of mesmerism shocks you with his much ado about nothing, but is

satisfied to take his fee and retire. The secret mental assassin stalks abroad, and needs to be branded to be known in what he is doing. Why we take so few students is because of the great danger there is in promiscuously teaching metaphysics, or the power of mind to do good, lest it abuse that trust, forsake metaphysics, and this developed mental power becomes the steam of physics and the extracts and essences of evil. I shudder when I remember that God is just and see a student of metaphysics dare, for the petty consideration of money, teach his slight knowledge, and perhaps his want of it, to all whom he can obtain for hearers, even when he knows of the danger of doing this before the community is prepared for self-defence. Since ever we have been in the metaphysical field we have had but a little over two hundred pupils, and but three of these are known malpractitioners; and never but one of our students have yet passed the change called death.

The hue of the individual mind is reflected on the patient. The effects of the truth he utters and the error he indulges are both communicated from the practitioner, and their effect on the sick tells which predominates. The sick cannot afford to risk the effects of mesmerism because it has appeared to help them. What is termed material poisons produce present relief, but you admit they are dangerous in the final result. There are certain self-evident facts; this is one of them: that whoever practises the metaphysics we teach, through which the divine Mind pours in upon the age light and healing, cannot malpractise.

As metaphysics is understood, the thoughts that mortal mind embraces — envy, malice, hate, etc. — will be laid bare, and the evil intent cannot be hidden. We can even now plainly see the individual with the thought or evil intent that he sends forth; he cannot hide from us now when he is trying to produce sickness or work an evil result. Hence the strenuous arguments of the malpractitioner to separate us from our students to prevent the benefit of this knowledge being communicated to them; and the more confidence he has in his power to injure them if he succeeds in doing it. If he can keep one ignorant of what he is trying to do, and with his arguments make them believe he is not trying to influence his thoughts and conclusions, the mesmerist is satisfied to work on, having faith in the results.

There is another evil prevailing in our land, to which it is our duty to allude; namely, the ignorant verdict of clairvoyance. We would not be understood as censuring the individual, but the mistake. None should suppose the guessing of this class harmless, or that their descriptions and private verdict, perhaps imperiling the character, the liberty, or life of a fellow being, has no effect upon the community. The evidence or testimony of clairvoyance is not reliable, being based on the uncertain foundation of mortal beliefs and opinions, and governed by other minds instead of fixed facts.

The evidence was clear that mind alone killed the felon on whom the Oxford students experimented twenty-five years ago. This evidence of the power that mind exercises over the body has accumulated in weight and clearness until it culminates at this period in scientific statement and proof. Our courts recognize the evidence that goes to prove the committal of a crime; then, if it be clear that the mind of one mortal has killed another, is not the mind proved a murderer, and shall not the man be sentenced whose mind, with malice aforethought, kills? His hands, without mind to aid them, could not murder; but it is proven that his mind, without the aid of his hands, has killed. Our courts examine, judge, and sentence mind, not matter. Our legislators enact laws to govern mind, not matter, to restrain evil in the mind of man, to prevent it from deeds of violence, and to punish those deeds. To say, then, that our courts have no jurisdiction over mind contradicts precedents and admits their power limited to matter, and mind an outlaw that defies justice. But, we ask, can matter commit a crime, can matter be punished, and can you separate mind from that over which our courts hold jurisdiction? Mortal mind, and not matter, is the criminal in every case, and law defines, and the court sentences, crime according to the motive.

18

Those words of Judge Parmenter, at the decision of a case in Boston, are destined to become historic. He said: "I see no reason why metaphysics are not as important to medicine as to mechanics or mathematics." The crimes committed mentally are drifting the age towards self-defence; we hope the method it adopts will be more humane than in periods past. The re-establishment of the Christian era, or the mediaeval period of metaphysics, will be one of moderation and peace; but the reinauguration of this period will be met with demonology, or the unlicensed cruelty of mortal mind, that will compel mankind to learn metaphysics for a refuge and defence. Then shall be fulfilled the Scripture, "The wrath of man shall praise Thee, and the remainder thereof Thou shalt restrain." The individual who employs his developed mental powers, like an escaped felon, to commit atrocities according to opportunity, is safe at no period. God hath laid his hand upon him, justice is manacling him. Behold the cloud "no bigger than a man's hand," rising in the horizon of Truth, to pour down upon his guilty head the hailstones of doom. The millstones of envy and malice are weighing down that mortal mind to the depths of its evil nature, where the cankering chains of sin will hold it until suffering balances the account, loosens their cold clasp, subdues the perverse will, and quenches in agony the fires of remorse. Aggravation of error foretells its doom, repeating the pagan opinion, "Whom the gods destroy they first make mad."

From physics to metaphysics is full many a league in the line of light, but from the use of inanimate drugs to pass to the misuse of mortal mind, is to drop from the platform of manhood into the mire of folly and iniquity. To reckon against the course of honesty and humility is to push against the current that runs heavenward. Let the age that sits in judgment on the occult science of Mind sanction only such methods as are demonstrable science, and classify with St. Paul, — Now the works of the flesh are manifest, which are these: adultery, fornication, idolatry, variance, emulations, wrath, WITCHCRAFT.

ANIMAL MAGNETISM

by

Adam H. Dickey

Mrs. Eddy once wrote, "Teach your students what animal magnetism is; how it works in themselves and from outside sources on them. These are the points in which my students fail most in teaching; and are the most difficult to teach rightly so as not to frighten, but strengthen the student." Animal magnetism, as a term used in Christian Science, appertains to the human mind as it threatens man's spiritual thinking, and his ability to keep his thought undisturbed and fearless in his perfect protection against its "diabolical contrivances," as Mrs. Eddy once expressed it to Lady Victoria Murray. Why was Mrs. Eddy divinely led to use this term and to state: "This term is the most comprehensive and applicable one that possibly can be used for that which it represents." Why did she lay such stress on students being taught this subject in classes where one might think that a higher unfolding of Truth was the essential point to be set forth?

Man is spiritual and perfect at all times and a son of God, able to reflect infinite Mind. He is kept from the recognition and exercise of his normal freedom and his true selfhood by the claim of animal magnetism. From this it can be seen that the understanding of this claim, as well as the overcoming of it, constitutes the important teaching and practice of Christian Science. The claim must be uncovered; the assumption it makes to deceive must be set forth, as well as its character and purpose.

In *Science and Health with Key to the Scriptures* Mary Baker Eddy gives us a wonderful paragraph setting forth what one moment of divine consciousness signifies for man. "One moment of divine consciousness, or the spiritual understanding of Life and Love, is a foretaste of eternity. This exalted view, obtained and retained, when the Science of being is understood, would bridge over with life discerned spiritually the interval of death, and man would be in the full consciousness of his immortality and eternal harmony, where sin, sickness, and death are unknown."

How do we gain that one moment in Christian Science? It is not a moment that is the result of development, time, accretions or growth; but a point at which one has successfully freed his thought from the influence of animal magnetism, from the mesmerism that makes the unreal seem real and the real seem unreal. So that one moment comes as the result of a successful overcoming of animal magnetism in all its phases.

From this recognition comes the assurance that animal magnetism is not one of the rather unpleasant phases of experience that we must be taught to handle, and a part of class instruction that must be endured, but will soon be forgotten in the joy of the spiritual vision that floods in through a higher recognition of Deity; rather *it is the whole teaching.*

A ship that has a journey before it, needs ballast in order that it may not flounder under the action of the wind and waves. Students of Christian Science have a journey before them. What do the waves represent? What does the ballast represent? Does the ballast represent a knowledge of animal magnetism that enables us to keep an even keel as we sail through the waters of Truth? No. The waves represent animal magnetism and the ballast is our knowledge of Truth that enables us to keep an even keel on this perilous passage. If one does not like this portrayal of man's effort to win his salvation, let him turn back, because he is not fit for the kingdom of heaven.

Students rejoice in the lessons about God, when in reality those precious lessons are the ballast. They chemicalize over the lessons on animal magnetism when in reality these lessons represent the only knowledge that will enable man to free himself from bondage and so function as a son of God normally and naturally. Never forget, however, that a right representation of the subject of animal magnetism will cause the student to feel eager for the fray, and he will recognize it as a "good fight," as Paul describes it. He will recognize that its devilishness comes because it is not understood. Let no teacher or student of Christian Science cease from emphasizing the importance of handling this claim, since a knowledge of it is the greatest gift of Christian Science to humanity and Mrs. Eddy's grandest offering to posterity.

Following are eighteen reasons why Mrs. Eddy was led to use the term animal magnetism. God led her to use it in order to:

1. Conceal from mortal mind the knowledge of itself, that might lead to an abuse of man's mental powers.
2. Enable us to handle evil separated from all sense of law, origin, reputation, or history.
3. Drive the student to overcome error with Truth, an effort which represents spiritual development, which is the true blessing which Christian Science offers and fosters.
4. Relieve God of all responsibility for the origin, activity, or manifestation of evil.
5. Enable man to handle evil separated from man, hence, as an impersonal claim.
6. Translate evil into a form that can be recognized as nothing.
7. Indicate that evil operates as cause wholly in a mental realm, and so must be handled mentally.
8. Provide the student with a fighting word that will arouse him to instant resistance, so that he will never let error go unhandled.
9. Prove that evil is always fightable in cause, no matter what its effect may be.

10. Show that error operates by putting a glamour, or magnetism of desirability over the animal sense that is in reality wholly undesirable and mortal.

11. Show that man's endeavors to overcome evil must broaden to cover both pain and pleasure, both human discord and human harmony, both the wolf and the wolf magnetized or glamoured, to appear attractive or harmless in sheep's clothing.

12. Show that error works entirely mesmerically through suggestion.

13. Indicate that the error that assails us is not aimed at us personally, but is aimed at the Truth. Hence, we feel it because we have pledged ourselves to support, defend and to embody the Truth.

14. Reveal that the underlying purpose of error is not to harm man as effect, to make him suffer, or even to kill him, but to separate him from God, to interfere with his reflection of God; and, since God is man's life, this effort marks animal magnetism as a mental assassin or mental murderer.

15. Impress upon thought the constant necessity for keeping alert to the claim of evil without being afraid of it. Man should never go to sleep over the danger of the claim unhandled, only fear lest he go to sleep to the necessity for constant watchfulness. ANIMAL MAGNETISM UNHANDLED ALWAYS HANDLES YOU. The warfare with evil is no child's play, even if it is waged in Christian Science with the weapon, or recognition, that because God is All, evil is nothing. Awake to its claims, man is safe. Asleep to them, he is in danger.

16. Present the human mind in such a form, with a handle that the student can grasp and thereby overthrow it. A smooth door without a handle could not be opened. The moment a handle is put on it, you can grasp the handle and pull the door open. Hence, through the use of the term animal magnetism, Mrs. Eddy has revealed man's adequate capacity to resist evil in such a way that it will no longer stand between him and God.

17. Enable the student to detect or perceive ends from beginnings as far as error is concerned. Suppose you were about to plant a seed in your garden; what a protection it would be to have someone who would label it deadly poison before you went through the miserable process of planting and tending it to the point where you discovered it for yourself! The term animal magnetism enables the student to label even a harmless-seeming suggestion in its incipiency with the same accuracy that others would be able to employ only after it was developed to full maturity. You might save the life of a man who had a cobra's egg in his house, if you could label it a cobra before it hatched. So the term animal magnetism labels suggestions lust, murder, death, in their incipient stages. Mrs. Eddy used the term animal magnetism to put the mark of the beast on what otherwise might appear harmless, and even worth retaining and cultivating.

18. Explain the true meaning of the fear of the Lord as recognition of the deadliness of the human mind in all its phases, and hence, the vital necessity for handling it, since it is malicious mischief which God demands us to reduce to nothingness. The student needs this impulse of the fear of the Lord to rouse him to the mental activity necessary to throw off this claim, although Mrs. Eddy's teachings furnish us with the calm, confident consciousness that through divine Mind we are always master of the claim; that it can never conquer us because, armed with divine power and understanding, we are invulnerable. "Love is the liberator," she tells us. Evil is a menace only because of our belief in it. Destroy man's belief in it and it falls. Then God is seen as ALL.

The Children of Israel were walking through the desert of animal magnetism and the manna represented a knowledge of Truth that sustained them each day. The manna had little to do with the journey except as being necessary to sustain them. They had not made a demonstration that would have given them a knowledge of animal magnetism; that is why they were not ready for the promised land and stayed back through fear of the children of Anak, who represented that claim of animal magnetism. Egypt stands for darkness, or animal magnetism.

The prodigal son took the truth that was his and went down, investigated, and surmounted this claim and returned to the father's house fully equipped to function without interference as a child and son of God. The older brother was content to be sustained by his knowledge of the truth in his father's house and never attained the precious knowledge of the hidden workings of evil that his brother had. Not valuing this knowledge he could not understand the joy that it brought to all to have had someone go down and probe this nefarious falsity and thereby master and destroy it.

This parable shows the shipwreck awaiting students who, loving the sweet revealings of Truth that Christian Science brings, prefer to be sustained by that and feed on it year after year, and so, although they are long on the knowledge of Truth, they are short on the knowledge of the hidden ways of evil in accomplishing iniquity.

Likewise the Children of Israel illustrate those who having made the splendid preliminary demonstration of being fed with the bread of Truth, do not go farther and obtain a knowledge of the operations of evil.

One of the first revealings that comes to a student who determines to gain this understanding of animal magnetism, is that animal magnetism endeavors to reverse the student's estimate of the importance of a knowledge of evil as compared with that of a knowledge of Truth. The former is held up as inconsequential and the latter as the all-in-all of Christian Science. Yet of what value is the vessel all properly balanced with ballast if it does not set out upon its journey over the waves of error?

FORMS OF ANIMAL MAGNETISM DEFINED

by

Harry I. Hunt

Question: Please explain the difference between *animal magnetism, aggressive mental suggestion*, and *malicious malpractice*, and help us see how to handle them successfully.

Answer: First of all, do not flinch at the term *animal magnetism.* Mrs. Eddy tells us in *Science and Health* that this is "the specific term for error, or mortal mind." This is the most exact scientific term we have for evil, or error, and its operation. Animal magnetism is the sum total of error, as the seven devils: *envy, sensuality, malice, hate, revenge, anger*, resulting from *fear*. We find there is nothing to fear. These are not qualities of Mind; they never have been expressed by Mind; hence, they cannot be reflected by man. Whatever assails your sonship with God, is a belief of a carnal or animal so-called mind, maliciously arguing against your perfection, your understanding, your knowledge of healing, your indissoluble connection with God. Do not fear this argument. It has no power, no source, no channel, no object, no manifestation. As a mindless belief, it is without effect, without law. You can annul it by knowing that you do not have to believe this belief; you are not under it; you can not be mesmerized into believing it and you know it. This knowledge dissolves fear and assures victory. You always perceive what you know because you can only see your own thoughts. Realization and demonstration are one.

At one time a student who visited Mrs. Eddy brought her small daughter along. When it came time to leave, they were invited to ride with Mrs. Eddy in the carriage to the train. Mrs. Eddy asked Mr. Frye not to ride along State Street where the trolleys run. The little girl whispered to her mother and asked if Mrs. Eddy was afraid of the cars? The mother whispered back, "Ask her yourself." So the child asked the question. Mrs. Eddy explained that the horses, Dolly and Princess, were not accustomed to the clatter of the electric cars. She didn't want them frightened, adding (exact quote), "I NEVER ANSWER THE CALL OF ANIMAL MAGNETISM."

Aggressive mental suggestion, the lie, is the voice of malicious animal magnetism attempting to reverse the truth about yourself. If you declare yourself the perfect sinless child of God, the lie further suggests that you are a child of evil, unworthy to be called the child of God. The lie further suggests that you are a Christian Scientist who is incapable of knowing and using the truth about man, that will deliver you from this fabrication of lies. You never can fail to detect this lie, expose it and destroy it, because it is always manifested as *doubtful or confused thought*. Truth brings us certainty and peace, and leads us out of this *false animal sense*. There is no power, no mind back of this false sense. The only power is good, and there is nothing created of which you ever need to be afraid. As Paul has written, "God hath not given you the spirit of fear, but of power, and of love, and of a sound mind."

Mental malpractice is defined by Mrs. Eddy in *Miscellaneous Writings* as "a bland denial of Truth, and is the antipode of Christian Science." A *bland denial* is one that puts you to sleep or makes you apathetic in defense of the Truth of being. Where does this denial operate? Only in your own thought. Some of the most common forms of mental malpractice are: to prophesy evil or accident; to express fear; to credit another with malice, envy, hatred or resentment; to see another as a malpractitioner; to give reasons for a failure to heal; to accept evil as true for oneself or for another; to criticize our neighbor. The law is "Thou shalt love thy neighbor as thyself." Any mental transgression of this law is mental malpractice, always operating within the arena of your own thought. It can therefore be readily corrected and healed and so annulled.

Malicious mental practice is the suggestion that somebody is hating me. If I accept the suggestion, I take hatred into my thought as a reality of the Mind which is infinite Love. To annul this claim I must know that it is only what is in my thought that can harm me. If I see a hater, I must suffer for seeing or believing that which is not an expression of Love. That which does not manifest Love has no existence, no consciousness. Man exists at the focus of infinite Love. He is never out of focus, therefore never absent from infinite Love nor conscious of its opposite. The annulment of all these mesmeric claims of mortal mind is in knowing that all being, all consciousness, is of God, and is good. There is no God of hatred. All is Love; there is no hate.

You must save your Christ-child. Every time you give a treatment fearing it will not work, you become a Pharoah seeking to destroy the new born babe.

When a claim continues after you have destroyed your belief in it, it is because of universal belief. It is not always enough to destroy personal belief in evil. We must cease believing that others believe in evil. All evil is specific and universal belief, and it should be handled from both viewpoints. We must not only heal our belief about ourselves, but we also must heal our belief of other's belief about us as well.

WISER THAN SERPENTS

(From *The Christian Science Journal*, March, 1925)

by

Dr. John M. Tutt

It may said that much of the trouble in the world comes from failure to handle animal magnetism. Since it is the necessity of Christians to imitate the example of Christ Jesus, it follows that Christians have the inescapable duty of proving the unreality of the works of the devil. Now the works of the devil, evil, may be said in a general way to be comprised in the suppositious activities of mortal mind. Only when the so-called human mind yields to divine wisdom, to the government of the one divine Mind, God, does it awaken from the mesmeric dream of evil thoughts and deeds. Christian Scientists, who are in a measure aroused from this hypnosis, are proportionately capable of overcoming evil in themselves and in others.

Animal magnetism is a name for evil in its false claim to be and to do something; it is the belief of evil in action. Wherever a falsity claims to be exerting itself to be and to do, there is animal magnetism. In *Science and Health* Mrs. Eddy gives *animal magnetism* as a definition of *serpent.*

The word "serpent" appears early in the Scriptures, and throughout both the Bible and *Science and Health*. It is employed as the most adequate type of evil. From the statement regarding it in Genesis, it has stood for what Paul defined as the "deceivableness of unrighteousness." "Now the serpent was more subtile than any beast of the field which the Lord God had made," we are told, and the Scriptural narrative presents the qualities of the serpent as

29

subtlety, duplicity, venom, adroitness, cunning, charm, fear, hate, anger, the counterfeit of wisdom. The serpent is represented as engendering fear. It claims to terrorize, fascinate, and kill. It is supposed to produce and transmit poison. Its entire activity claims to be destructive; and this characteristic remands it to the realm of the unreal, to the sphere of the nonexistent; for that which is destructive or destructible cannot really continue even to seem to exist — it carries within itself the elements of oblivion.

The one quality ascribed to the serpent that would seem to have reality is wisdom. To be sure, adroitness and charm have also better meanings, and when, together with wisdom, they are considered spiritually, they are properly attributable to the serpent of God's creating, of which Mrs. Eddy writes in *Science and Health,* "The serpent of God's creating is neither subtle nor poisonous, but is a wise idea, charming in its adroitness, for Love's ideas are subject to the Mind which forms them, — the power which changeth the serpent into a staff."

The use of the word "wisdom" as applied to the mortal mind sense of serpent is similar to Jesus' reference to the wisdom of this world. He said, "The children of this world are in their generation wiser than the children of light." Here wisdom has more the qualities of prudence and discretion. Jesus commended these qualities, and said to his disciples, "Behold, I send you forth as sheep in the midst of wolves: be ye therefore wise as serpents, and harmless as doves."

In *Miscellaneous Writings* Mrs. Eddy has amplified what the Master said at that time, by declaring that the "wisdom of a serpent is to hide itself." We are, then, to obey the injunction of the Master by hiding ourselves from error's inspection and action, which are always with intent to harm and destroy. Mrs. Eddy has also declared in her *Message to The Mother Church for 1902,* "It is wise to be willing to wait on God, and to be wiser than serpents."

Since the serpent here is a synonym of all active evil or animal magnetism, we have need to be wiser than animal magnetism. In the allegory of the Garden of Eden, the serpent is represented as talking to Eve. Mrs. Eddy reminds us that there is no such thing in animal life as a talking snake. The talking serpent used Eve's tongue, for it had no ability to talk itself. Evil may even, fraudulently, take the livery of heaven. The serpent talked to Eve in terms of her own thinking and speech. Indeed, any evil belief comes to us in the guise of our own thought. It can come in no other way, since we see, feel, hear, touch, and taste only what we believe. Thus all these evil things depend for their seeming reality upon our acceptance of them at the behest of mortal mind.

Now the question arises, How can a talking serpent hide itself? Will not its speech inevitably betray it even if behind a camouflage of words? According to Paul, "the god of this world" — the devil, evil, animal magnetism, the original talking serpent — is "dishonesty . . . craftiness, . . . handling the word of God deceitfully." Beware the smooth talker, who hides behind the words of truth, the lying maker of the venom of malice and mischief. There is little to choose between the venom producer and the venom vender, carrying and spreading the poison of gossip, scandal mongering, idle talk, malicious criticism.

"The wisdom of a serpent is to hide itself;" and because the serpents of error come to us in the guise of thought, and can come in no other way, therefore the serpent hides itself in our own thinking. We must seek for it there. The animal magnetism outside our own consciousness can never harm us. The wisdom of the serpent is to hide itself by masquerading as good, as having created reality. For this reason, the serpent is a type of hypocrisy "with all deceivableness of unrighteousness."

This animal element, which claims to be inherent in mortals, impels them to all evil in the name of good. Animal subtleties are deceived and deceiving, but to themselves alone. Paul wrote to the Corinthians, "I fear, lest by any means, as the serpent beguiled Eve through his subtilty, so your minds should be corrupted from the simplicity that is in Christ." This simplicity in Christ, Truth, enables one to break the mesmeric charm of matter's seemingly pleasant aspects, and to antidote the hypnotic virus of matter's ugly phases.

In displaying its so-called wisdom, the serpent hides itself in the most effective place for hiding, namely, a hole. The superficial student hesitates or stops short at the hole of the serpent. He loves to think of God as Love, but he dislikes to stir up a nest of serpents. He will not handle animal magnetism. He either does not see the error or, seeing it, does not want to or will not deny it, reverse it, and reject it.

The true Scientist boldly turns the serpent out of its hole. He does this with the wisdom of God and not with his own human mentality however. Thus he emulates our Leader's counsel and example to be "wiser than serpents." To be "wiser than serpents" is to employ the wisdom of God, the one divine Mind, in bringing the serpent out of its hiding place or hole, handling it, and taking away its sting. Thus handled — that is, reversed with Truth — the lie or serpent becomes a staff on which to lean. Note that to be wiser than a serpent is to employ the wisdom of God, not of one's self. No one can, of his own belief in mortal mind or will, uncover error. The true Scientist lets Truth uncover error. The lie uncovered, the student should destroy it, but only by replacing it with the truth. All animal magnetism is a supposititious reversal of the divine activity of Christ, or Truth. As has been previously implied, the serpent, when reversed in Science, becomes a staff on which to lean. If we allow Truth to uncover error, we shall find the serpent replaced by a staff. We must be active in allowing Truth to uncover the lie; we must be insistent and persistent. God must do this; but we must see to it that we are witnesses to Truth's activity.

Jesus said, "I am not come to destroy, but to fulfil." May

not this be taken to mean, I am not come to destroy reality, but to restore it to consciousness? If we handle the serpent of materialism with the wisdom of God, we shall realize, proportionately to our right activity, the allness of Spirit and spiritual things. Christian Science is not destructive, but restorative. Not even the serpent itself is lost in reversion, but it thus becomes a type of true wisdom.

All too often the hole of the asp is to be found in one's own bosom. Such a hiding place seems most immune from attack. People are usually more willing to invade the nest of error in another's thought and heart, and sometimes without the wisdom of God, than to dig out the nests of evil within their own thinking, a process which requires greatest courage. It is natural for a Christian Scientist to handle serpents. Jesus said of his disciples that they should do so unharmed; and a Christian Scientist who does not handle animal magnetism, and handle it with divine omnipotence, is not a genuine disciple of Christ or a worthy follower of his Leader. It is unnatural for a Christian Scientist to ignore the serpents or their hiding places. One should use discretion, and be sure of his ability to accomplish what he would do for Christ. How can one be sure of his ability, capacity, and competency? By preparedness. If the student does his daily work effectively against animal magnetism, he will find that the work on any specific case will become more and more incidental. He should remember that while the rattlesnake heralds his offensive, most serpents are quiet, striking without warning; hence the necessity to be impervious and immune to their poison. The antidote for all serpent bites is spiritual thinking and living; for spiritual sense alone can immunize against the mesmerism of the beliefs of matter.

To be "wiser than serpents" is also to be undeceived by hidden sin. Conversely, we should be wise as serpents in hiding our aims and plans from mortal mind. The serpent is wise enough to attempt to hide its venom, its presence and purpose. We should be wise to detect, attack, and destroy the serpent with its supposititious virus. We should cultivate perception, initiative, and spontaneity in handling evil. Our leader tells us that the illusion of Moses regarding the serpent lost its power to alarm him when he reached out and conquered his fear.

In one of the pictures in *Christ and Christmas* Mrs. Eddy places the serpent behind the woman. Jesus said, "Get thee behind me, Satan." King Hezekiah sang, "Thou hast cast all my sins behind thy back." Paul declared that he was intent upon "forgetting those things which are behind." A lie is never true; the unreal does not exist. Jesus knew this, and feared not animal magnetism; otherwise, he could not have put the serpent behind him. But note! Jesus commanded Satan, the lie, to get behind him. He handled the serpent of animal magnetism — but as nothing, and with the power of Truth.

Nothing can substitute the Christ and spiritual consciousness. Beware the serpent of materialism hiding its purpose to destroy both individual lives and usefulness and the existence and usefulness of the movement of Christian Science by magnifying the supposititous material in the place of or in the guise of the spiritual. There is no kinship between the material and the spiritual. If we protect evil beliefs by our approval and indulgence, tacitly or openly, the consequent multiplication of the serpent's progeny will increase our pains and regrets. If we concede room to one devil, we may find seven others come to share its abode in our consciousness.

These serpents, or animal magnetism, are not people or things, even though mortal mind does claim to operate as mortal men and things. These serpents are, one and all, just false concepts — material beliefs. The serpent we handle for ourselves, we at the same time handle impersonally for others — indeed, for all mankind — because Christ, Truth, which heals and saves anybody, truly heals and saves everybody. Can we not visualize that happy day when "the wolf also shall dwell with the lamb, and the leopard shall lie down with the kid; . . . and the sucking child shall play on the hole of the asp, and the weaned child shall put his hand on the cockatrice' den;" when "they shall take up serpents; and if they drink any deadly thing, it shall not hurt them"? And why? Because they shall be "wise as serpents," yea, they shall be "wiser than serpents." Then "they shall not hurt nor destroy in all my holy mountain: for the earth shall be full of the knowledge of the Lord, as the waters cover the sea."

THE IMPERSONAL NATURE OF EVIL

(From the *Christian Science Sentinel,* October 17, 1903)

by

Blanche Hersey Hogue

For generations the trend of human education has divided the world into two great classes, good people and bad people. Much of the religious teaching of the past has classified humankind as saved or lost, without reference to individual merit, but rather because of a definite foreordained plan. The liberality of modern religious thought gives to the individual the opportunity to effect his salvation through the choice of righteousness, but still draws its line between good and bad people. Advancing thought has rebelled in great measure against extreme classification, for the very evident reason that good people are often found guilty of startling inconsistencies, while the so-called evil people have been moved by noble impulses to the performance of great and good deeds. Theoretically a dividing line could be drawn, but in practice it could not be made to adjust itself to the men and women whose lives it attempted to classify.

However, progressive thought, obeying an instinctive love of good, has been rapidly outgrowing this narrower interpretation of the human problem, and has encouraged the cultivation of good and the destruction of evil in every life, trusting the outcome to the wisdom of a loving Father. Education has pressed forward upon broadening lines, until the advent of the Science of Christianity in Mrs. Eddy's book, *Science and Health with Key to the Scriptures,* has given to the world an interpretation of human conditions which removes the question of good and evil from the domain of person to the realm of mind.

It is readily discerned that the Master's illustrations of the wheat and tares, the sheep and the goats, are of little ethical value today unless the disciple applies them to his own good and evil thinking, rather than to the fate of good and bad people. The perplexing question of who shall be saved and who shall be lost, resolves itself into the question of what shall be saved and what shall be lost, and as the world recognizes the eternity and indestructibility of good, and the perishable and passing nature of evil, every man's right to achieve permanent right thinking, and consequently permanent salvation, will be established.

A practical illustration of the impersonal nature of evil and the scientific method of its destruction, was given once by a Christian Scientist in conversation with a man who declared that he did not wish to know Christian Science if it insisted upon his loving his enemies. The question was asked him: "If a man throws a stone at you and hurts you, and you wish to avoid a repetition of the occurrence, would you turn upon the stone? No, certainly not. You would attack the man who threw it."

Another question followed: "If thought of malice or hate or jealousy picks up a man and throws him at you, would you attack the man? Is he not just the stone in the hands of the evil impulse which overpowered him, and would you not deal with the thoughts which threw him at you?"

This illustration suggests that thought is the actor in every case, and that the man through whom the action occurs is but the instrument of an evil tendency. According to the illustration we are confronted not by an evil person, but by one who knows not how to protect himself from the pressure of the evil impulse, and who consequently becomes its tool. The person who has not the strength to resist doing that which harms his brother, is a greater victim to the evil than is the injured one, for he is more directly under the control of evil, and so more in need of deliverance.

And what is the mode of deliverance for the man thrown

as well as the man injured? In our illustration, the stones nearest at hand may be removed from the pathway, but if the impulse of the thrower is not checked, he will readily find other stones suited to his purpose.

If, however, the evil tendency itself be destroyed, stones may be all about him, and yet not used to another's harm. The illustration applies directly to the mental situation, for in the adjustment of all difficulties we deal not with man, but with qualities of thought; not with persons, but with the impulses which actuate them.

The individual Christian Scientist obtains his deliverance from the action of evil by refusing to give evil the approval and support of his own thought. He not only refuses, so far as he can, to indulge in evil himself; but furthermore refuses to believe that any other child of God can be made an avenue for such indulgence. *He separates man from evil, and attacks evil as the one common enemy which seeks to find expression through every man.* When sin is no longer able to act in and through a person, it can no longer injure others through him. The individual may remain associated with others as before, but he has gained such mastery over evil that it can no longer hurl him at his fellow-man.

If the student of Christian Science works quietly and patiently with his own thought, refusing to give the power to evil which comes through another as faithfully as he would refuse to entertain it himself, he is separating himself from evil, and lessening its influence upon his own life and indirectly the lives of those who would harm him. To the one who possesses this measure of enlightenment, every attempted injury becomes a blessing, for it compels him to find refuge in this impersonal attitude of thought, and so exalts him. It disarms his temptation to show resentment as nothing else can, for it interests him in the accomplishment of the other man's deliverance as well as his own. He finds himself warring, not with his brethren, but with the evil which tries to entangle all men, and as he wars successfully, overcoming evil with good, he will say with Paul: "If God be for us, who can be against us."

HANDLING ANIMAL MAGNETISM

(From *The Christian Science Journal,* August, 1943)

by

Fredda R. Gratke

A Christian Scientist who for many years had proved for herself the power of divine Mind to dissolve human discords, found herself overcome by an illness that seemed to resist the application of Truth.

Praying earnestly for enlightenment, she was led to open the textbook, *Science and Health,* where she read, "When the mechanism of the human mind gives place to the divine Mind, self-ishness and sin, disease and death, will lose their foothold." The words "mechanism of the human mind" arrested her attention.

Christian Science had taught her that God is divine Mind, Spirit, Soul, Principle, Life, Truth and Love; that all that this infinite Mind creates is eternal, harmonious and spiritual; that what seems baneful, evil or transitory is the product of a false sense of things, the phenomenon of unreal mortal thinking. But what is "the mechanism of the human mind"? Earnestly she searched consciousness, and through the illumination that came from her reaching out for divine Mind's answer, she saw the secret of certain phases of wrong mental activity, or animal magnetism.

Animal magnetism is nothing to fear. It is only another term for mortal mind, or error, and should never be thought of as anything else. Mrs. Eddy gives us this clear definition in *Science and Health*: "As named in Christian Science, animal magnetism or hypnotism is the specific name for error, mortal mind. It is the false belief that mind is in matter, and is both evil and good; that evil is as real as good and more powerful. This belief has not one quality of Truth." To handle animal magnetism in Christian Science is to see its unreal nature on the basis that all reality is in God and His idea. It is heartening to realize that when its mesmeric arguments are silenced, we find there is nothing left to be handled, for error cannot attach itself to spiritual-mindedness.

The student realized that in connection with the problem with which she was then concerned, the mesmeric mechanism, or animal magnetism, seemed to be operating in three ways: to hold thought to her past experiences, to imaginary pictures of her future, and to human reasoning about her problems of the present.

Her thoughts had involuntarily kept turning to past mistakes, injustices, unhappy experiences. But reasoning according to Christian Science, she knew that none of the sorrow, the disappointments, or discords had ever been part of real being, of Life or Love. Life is God, good. Therefore, if the past experiences had no good, nothing of God expressed in them, they had no Life in them, no Truth, no Love. Only to the extent that they remained in consciousness to annoy and fester, to that extent alone had "selfishness and sin, disease and death" found a foothold.

It was seen that even as the past is but a dream, and never had a place in God's radiant reality, so the imaginary pictures of an undesirable condition in the future had no basis in Principle. These pictures could come into consciousness only through suggestion of fear, of outlining, or of daydreaming. If they came as a suggestion of apprehension of possible evil, surely trust in God was lacking, for the omnipresence of infinite Love ensures that the sunlight of God's goodness will shine in every tomorrow, even as the sun pours out its light as each day dawns. Understanding the omnipresence of divine Love casts out fear; and confidently leaving our tomorrows in the hands of the Father, we find the dark suggestive picture wiped out. To indulge in mere human planning for the future holds thought in bondage, and interferes with the normal unfoldment of good from the operation of Principle. Daydreaming is no part of the divine knowing, and when mortal mind's outlining ceases, and consciousness confidently rests in the omnipotence of good, the infinite resources of divine Mind become increasingly apparent.

God lives in the eternal now, and moment by moment man's thoughts should reflect divine Mind's activity. How often we waste time in mentally talking to people who perhaps are not even present, explaining, excusing, justifying, and condemning, sending forth a stream of thought that can only attract a similar stream of error, creating in the mental realm a miniature unseen warfare.

The habit of holding mental conversations about error with ourselves or another, weaves a dark curtain of mortal thinking through which Love's healing light cannot penetrate. This type of argument robs those who indulge in it of their peace of mind, inspiration, and poise. It is not only wrong to the individual to whom the silent argument is directed, but even more detrimental to the one arguing. To see man as God sees him, to realize the impersonal nature of whatever error claims to govern in either ourselves or another, is to put peace and blessing in place of personal conflict.

Many times during the months of pain, the temptation had come to this individual to attribute an erroneous condition to malpractice or to the wrong thinking of others; but finally it was realized that she was the principle culprit in consenting to accept the aggressive arguments of evil and in believing that they were her identity and consciousness. At first it was difficult to stop this false mental activity. It would slip in to argue in spite of vigilance; but just as darkness disappears when a light is turned on, so the erroneous mental action ceases as spiritual thinking takes its place.

Each temptation was met with a declaration of some truth, the "mechanism of the human mind" was silenced, and a listening attitude took the place of erroneous mental conversations — listening for the messages from the divine Mind, the angels that are always near us and are heard as soon as evil's suggestions are hushed. When the mastery over mortal mind was gained in a goodly degree, the physical healing came, and with it a glorious sense of the availability of divine Love's impartation.

Jesus said, "Except ye . . . become as little children, ye shall not enter into the kingdom of Heaven." The child-consciousness dwells in joyous appreciation of present moments, unconcerned by past or future events. And how the world needs this carefree joy of the consciousness that basks in the sunlight of God's ever-present Love, a consciousness purified of materiality and inspired by the recognition of the kingdom of God at hand!

The great truths of Christian Science can be spiritually discerned only through the lens of purified thinking. These simple truths, firmly held to, lift thought to conscious at-one-ment with divine Love, bringing instantaneous healing.

If to gain control of our thinking necessitates righteous warfare, let us remember Mrs. Eddy's words from *Miscellaneous Writings*, "Be of good cheer; the warfare with one's self is grand." It is grand because through victory over self we are enabled to help others and are equipped to withstand the aggressive animal magnetism or evil suggestions abroad in the world today. Vision is cleared to behold that the kingdom of heaven is indeed here. In this kingdom man is seen manifesting perfect health, joy, and abundant supply. The dark curtain woven of wrong thinking had been rent by the sword of Truth, letting in the light of divine Mind and bringing to the individual consciousness the surety that "the Lord God omnipotent reigneth."

RECOGNIZING ONE'S ENEMY

by

Samuel Greenwood

Naturally the first step toward defeating one's enemy is to recognize who or what he is, since not to know this enemy is to be in danger of coming under his control. That one's enemies are not persons, was made plain by Christ Jesus, when he commanded his followers to love those who manifest enmity toward them. In her illuminating article, "Love Your Enemies," found in *Miscellaneous Writings*, Mrs. Eddy writes, "Simply count your enemy to be that which defiles, defaces, and dethrones the Christ-image that you should reflect." We have here an infallible rule whereby at all times we may detect our enemy, never as a person, but as an evil animus or influence, a false mental argument that, if accepted, would alienate us from our highest sense of good.

The only personal enemy we can have, is our own false sense of personality, as Mrs. Eddy points out in this article. Others may think they cherish enmity towards us and be willing to do us harm, but that is of less moment to us than our own mental attitude. When we are conscious of entertaining no sense of personal enmity, we have a clear field whereon to meet and defeat the impersonal nature of error that would invade and defile one's consciousness. Only as these errors are stripped of their personality, even of our own, can we see them in their true light and intelligently begin the work of destroying them. Speaking of their enemies whom they were to meet in the land of Canaan, Moses enjoined upon the Israelites that they should "utterly destroy them," and "make no covenant with them, nor show mercy unto them." This should be wanton cruelty in a literal and personal sense; but when these enemies are metaphysically interpreted as the errors of belief that would keep humanity out of their spiritual heritage, we can see that a less absolute stand would only serve to perpetuate mankind's bondage to evil, as human history testifies.

What is it that would defile, deface and dethrone the Christ-image in our consciousness? Is it not whatever would rob us of our sense of spiritual good, spiritual love, and spiritual being? Such conditions are designated in the Scriptures as lusts of the flesh, or the qualities of the so-called "carnal mind"; and in *Science and Health* they are enumerated as lust, dishonesty, selfishness, envy, hypocrisy, slander, hate, etc. Who has not striven with one or more of these evils, seeking to make consciousness captive? Sometimes we may have failed in the conflict or have compromised with the enemy, only to struggle with shame and self-condemnation to regain our sense of freedom. If we have recognized that these are the enemies that we must encounter and overcome before we can fully realize the kingdom of heaven, we have made a hopeful beginning; but to deceive ourselves that one can make progress while showing mercy to or making covenants with them, by careless watching or half-hearted conflict, is a costly mistake.

One thing is certain — that when we have once fairly seen what our enemy is, it can never again enter in the guise of a friend, under the cloak of ignorance, or against our consent. If we are really awakened to the pernicious influence of anger, dishonesty, hate and all selfishness in defacing our concept of the perfect man, we cannot plead ignorance in admitting them again into our thought. If through selfish weakness or lack of moral courage we show mercy unto these enemies, it means that they have us captive, and that we shall have to pay "the uttermost farthing" for our release. Who that has seen the light of Christian Science, the absolute depravity of the claim of intelligent evil, in its various aliases, can continue innocently to give these place in the consciousness that should be "glory unto the Lord"?

(food for thought)

Grateful fact behind the
gratitude

the feel & know (the Word)
prayer - is) (Starting point
- being still
feeling; & healing
is being aware of Gods presence.

#645

Essential qualities
for extraordinary relationships

the feeling you have before
the symble —

— 800 - 8780525 —

Students of Christian Science who are practically applying its teachings, should know more of the nature and methods of so-called evil than do others. They should know its hideous deformities, the evidences of its devastating influence morally and physically. Yet so subtle are the claims of error that those who know best what it is, and who are in a measure aware of the demands of Truth, are still tempted day after day to think of evil as a person, to call it by name, to accept its evidence, and to carry out its suggestions. Human thought is ever ready to give intelligence to error by arguing with it as a person, as if it had voice and consciousness, although the student may persuade himself at the same time that he understands its impersonal nature. With all our experience as Christian Scientists, we are apt, without tireless vigilance, to walk into the enemies net by listening to audible error, giving back the angry word as if evil could talk or hear, instead of knowing its utter lack of being there at all, and thus grasping another opportunity to see the perfect man.

The moral of our experiences should be, that the enemy once recognized should always be treated as an enemy, and not that we should again come willingly under its yoke. When, for instance, we have seen the defiling influence of anger, why show it mercy when it again appears? Selfishness may argue that the resentful thought and cross word are easier than loving-kindness, and thus lead us to forget that we are not in this warfare for ease, but salvation. We behave more consistently in worldly affairs, for who would let into his counting-house or store one whom he knew by experience to be a thief? We take precaution against the loss of material things, while we carelessly leave our thought-doors open to every marauding error, as if the preservation of our consciousness were of less importance than the safety of our goods. Surely, if we let such mental conditions as hate, jealousy, revenge, dishonesty, and hypocrisy go on robbing us of our good thoughts, we cannot expect to progress in the understanding of the Science of God.

Why then do we let these acknowledged enemies into consciousness, when we know that their only influence is to deface and defile?

Not to be able to recognize error is, of course, to be in danger of mistaking it for the truth; but if one knows the truth, he cannot be deceived by its opposite. If we understand, even in part, that man is the image of God, we know that evil is no part of him, has no relation to him. Whatever would persuade us that evil is something, or that it is intelligently personal, is our enemy, no matter how relatively harmless its name may appear. If people now at strife, understand that their enemies are not people, they would not use material weapons in fighting them. If they had but known that their only enemies are greed, envy, jealousy, revenge, selfishness, and ambition, instead of persons, and that these wicked thoughts and motives were operating against them, not merely in the consciousness of their opponents but in their own, these terrible conflicts would never occur. Instead we should have the spectacle of nations striving and individuals striving with their own errors, whatever their nature, and not with one another, and conquering all evils in the name of Christ, the Son of God. It must sometime come to this, and the sooner Christian Scientists actually demonstrate in their own experience the reality and practicality of brotherly love and good will, the sooner will the vision of universal peace dawn upon mankind.

MENTAL MALPRACTICE

by

Dr. Franklin Morgan

Mental Malpractrice from Without

Thought transference comes through the physical senses so-called, and these senses compose all there is of a mortal. The idolatrous affection of a parent arousing in the child irritability, sensitiveness, often violent hatred or spasms of fear, is a good illustration of the reverse effect of mental influence.

The lower propensities of mortal mind, such as hatred, jealousy, envy, resentment, are not communicable as such. Rather they touch the thought of a relative or friend as worry, false sympathy or even grief, or they may depress or excite thought somewhat. The very nature of an erroneous character of thought is more or less exciting and always discordant to the one thinking it, and it therefore disturbs the rule of harmony or affection in him. Such thoughts are most harmful to the victim who indulges in evil thinking.

To believe that the thoughts of some person are responsible for our mistakes or sins or for our troubles or pains, is to secretly accuse and to cowardly condemn that person and also to commit the sin of malicious slander. Love one another. Think you that we can really love as Christ Jesus loved while we contemplate one single man, woman or child on earth of whom we are afraid or to whom we could refuse "a cup of cold water in His name?" Think you that we are loving and lovable when we fear the imaginary evil of pope or priest, Jew or Gentile, especially since we profess to know that "to fear anyone or anything is to hate that one or thing."

Mental Malpractice from Within

Mental malpractice is usually thought of as coming from without instead of within. That which we think of as human or mortal is spoken of as a belief. That which relates to Spirit we call an idea of Truth. An idea of Truth comes to us or appears in consciousness as a thought and its repeated appearance or recurrence may be termed divine influence.

But with thoughts or things that are discordant or due to sense testimony, we call them suggestions of error or malpractice; when they are insistent or persistent, we call them aggressive mental suggestion, because of their continual recurrence. This type of error is mistakenly called malpractice and is thought to come from without, or is the thought of some supposed person deliberately attempting to do us harm. Every experience of this type is due solely to a disturbed mentality within. Mrs. Eddy tells us in *Miscellaneous Writings*, "Suffering is self-inflicted." A disturbed mentality may continue or occur and reoccur until corrected by Truth. It may be forgotten, and thus remain latent in thought for hours or years, when it may be suddenly uncovered or recalled by reason of a suggestion. No matter how violent or persistent such suggestions may seem, they cannot be greater than the mentality which holds them, and therefore there is nothing to fear.

What is usually termed malicious mental malpractice comes from one's own thought or impressions of intense anger, jealousy, malice, envy, resentment, etc., of the past or present. This unfortunate state of belief is also called malicious aggressive suggestion and erroneously believed to come from without, from some person or persons whom the sinner imagines is deliberately attempting to assassinate him.

Look within to heal this condition. Look into the mirror of your own mentality where you will see the cause of your own self-inflicted wounds. "Cast the beam out of thine own eye." Learn what is in thine own mentality that is unlike God and cast it out.

Just so surely as we enter into the little or big things of daily life with a buoyant appreciation, praising and thanking God for the privilege of occupation — whatever it may be — just as surely will we heal and be healed, even without a conscious effort. It cannot possibly be difficult or fatiguing to thank God that error is not you or yours, me or mine. It cannot possibly injure mentally or physically to thank God that neither matter nor mortal man ever created anything or anyone, and that God made all in the perfection of Himself. It cannot possibly weary or disturb one to thank God that evil is a negation, a fraction of belief only, and is therefore without Truth or law. Once we learn to continually glorify God in our every thought and deed, there can never again appear any claim of mental weakness or bodily ills. Gratitude is God's law of healing and hence destroys all sense of discord or ills.

MORAL IDIOCY

Author Unknown

The trick of the antichrist these days is not so much attack, in its attempt to vanquish, but provocation — to provoke us out of at-one-ment with God, separate us from Soul, and thus render us powerless. It would incite us into a sense of human contention with moral idiocy — fooling us into a sense of things wherein unprincipled beliefs seem firmly entrenched, appearing and reappearing, receding and advancing, never letting up, bringing confusion, disorder, humiliation, frustration, and making us feel we are "getting nowhere."

The hatred of animal magnetism seems to send a claim of moral idiocy into our affairs which, in some way, we feel duty bound to respond humanly. Not recognizing it as evil's 'bait,' we take the claim into consciousness, listen to it, reason with it, try to figure it out, reform it, live with it, get along in spite of it, instead of seeing it as a decoy and turning at once to deal with the impersonal hatred itself (motivated by revenge, envy, jealousy, etc.) and casting it out by refusing to be fooled and diverted by its 'medium' — the deluded individual who apparently seems to feel nothing.

Through so-called 'good' qualities — personal responsibility, compassion, righteousness, integrity, human love — we feel *obligated* to listen to its arguments, put up with it. Too late do we begin to see what it is doing to us.

A kind of higher type of human nature — such as Job — has difficulty, in getting past this *duty stage*. Job believed that his health, happiness and peace depended on his ability to heal — convince and convert — the moral idiocy around him. When he found his own humility and saw that it was infinite, the duty sense fell naturally away, and he was healed.

So we, too, seem to play into the hands of hatred, falling into and perpetuating this claim of everlasting warfare. The antichrist sets up its phantasma of moral idiocy, and we retaliate. Thus we keep it going and seem to take on suffering of all kinds, as did Job — nervousness, worry, fear, loss, fatigue, inflammation, animosity, and separation. This is just what evil's hatred has been working for. It defies us to turn away instantly and completely from the false picture and cast out these immoral, perverted beliefs and so relax and be at peace. And, of course, personal sense, which cannot rise high enough to discern and uncover the real culprit, can never do so. The hatred claims to operate in this way because it is inert — nothing — unless there is conflict through the belief of duality. Why? Because, in the realm of belief, conflict is necessary to generate all forms of energy, destructive forces, power, heat, etc. Evil's hatred is generated by using moral idiocy suggestions as a means by which it can provoke, incense, challenge that human sense of astuteness and moral responsibility which sees it, but does not have the *unselfishness* or *humility* to refuse to deal with it and cast it out.

Evil's only hope for life and power then, in belief, is to keep the moral idiocy constantly in view by causing conflict. But does it keep it in view, or *do we*? In the world today, and in our own affairs, we must remember it is not so much the issue involved; it is the *disruption* that animal magnetism is striving for. Its whole game is to separate at-one-ment — Principle and idea, reasoning and discernment, noumenon and phenomenon, unfoldment and manifestation — and to keep us fighting. To do this it uses moral idiocy, directing it specifically towards the belief of human integrity and duty.

The human sense of ego has not discerned the fact that human good is able to destroy evil only insofar as it recognizes itself to be phenomenon, the unfoldment in thought and action of the one cause, Soul — which has already created everything perfect, whole,

51

faultless, and which forever operates from the standpoint of dominion. The belief of human integrity never emerges from the sense of struggle, and so chafes, frets, contends, staying in the realm of conflict and duality, never seeming to get out. Thus, the antichrist is perpetuated, in belief, as personal sense argues, debates, and tries to heal the moral idiocy — or tries to ignore it.

So what is it that conflicts with the hatred-directed beliefs of moral idiocy? Not humility, but some moral integrity which has not yet been raised to the level of divine Science — divine Love — and so feels maligned, persecuted, restricted, opposed. All moral idiocy has to do then, is to see to it that we believe some personal, virtuous "I am" belief about ourselves, one that is not yet raised to the level of the divine quality and power of humility. Then evil claims to send the specific moral idiotic belief that will conflict with it, for moral idiocy can find an opponent in personal sense, but not in humility. It can set up its field of duality only in a sense of self vs. self. For example, personal intelligence as opposed to unreasonableness; personal accomplishment as opposed to laziness; personal purity as opposed to corruption; personal righteousness as opposed to moral blindness; personal integrity as opposed to dishonesty; human will (as good) as opposed to evil intention, indifference, scorn; and personal wealth, beauty and human joy as opposed to lack, ugliness, depression.

Then are we going to fall into the trap? Let us recognize what the hatred is trying to do. Its whole game is to make us feel we are the victims of circumstances, to keep us fighting, to wear us out, by making us believe that the moral idiocy is doing something, is a terrible thing, is fooling everybody, is governing our lives, destroying our happiness, giving us a bad time, etc. In this way, evil keeps us involved through our human, moral, personal inability to let go, and so we never get to the root of the matter. Consequently, we never rise into the pure Christ-consciousness of at-one-ment, and demonstrate it completely right where we are.

Mrs. Eddy says to "save the victim of the mental assassin." Who is the victim? The moral idiot? *Or are we the victim through the so-called moral idiot?* If we save ourselves (that is, our pure, unadulterated, spiritual sense of ourselves) and so preserve divine Science, by knowing that hatred cannot touch us in any way through any tool of moral idiocy, the so-called idiot will learn the Truth in his own way, at the proper time for all concerned — whether he is a relative, employer, friend — and we do not want to spare him or deprive him of any of the lessons he is to learn according to how long he has let himself be used. Humility sees that this is up to God. Also, that the idea and its affairs can only be blessed.

The important thing to remember is that the antichrist is trying to disturb us — the loyal ones, the obedient ones; to get us to harbor a belief of something else besides good; to take on a false sense of responsibility for others to the extent of our own downfall, if it can. It would cast us down from humility or at-one-ment, and so render us powerless.

So we must refuse to be goaded, on the human level, taking only such footsteps as unfold through humility, leaving error to destroy itself, while the idea remains untouched, by reason of there being no battle, no opposite, no negative side. This consciousness is the only weapon with which to destroy hatred, *and animal magnetism knows this, or seems to.*

Humility takes us off the battlefield. Translating selfhood, personal joys, human volition, into Soul, and seeing that our human selfhood is only objectification of divine ideas manifested, this removes the target. From this standpoint, impersonal humility comfortably uncovers and casts out the demon of moral idiocy from the divine level, taking it out of our experience.

If we seem to be moved, incensed, irritated, affected in any way, by the seeming idiocy of someone, the hatred has accomplished the first step in its campaign. It has made us leave home ground, forget our real self — the one spiritual, infinite selfhood — and see another self somewhere. The minute we do this, we come down from at-one-ment, humility, our perfect Christ-consciousness, and dwell in a 'something else besides' state of thought.

So what must we do? Endeavor to see the other person as God's man? Consciously try to love him? Think about him at all? No. This is just what the antichrist hopes we will do. For this proves to it that it has gone unrecognized. Instead we should turn all the more to our own true selfhood and work for it. We should "gather ourselves up in God," and scientifically prove that our own true selfhood — our own infinite Christ-consciousness — is all the man there is, the *only* manifestation, in our affairs. From here, we are able to see the whole claim as impersonal moral idiocy coming from hatred of the Truth, which we must not argue with, but must cut off, turn away from and cast out. For it is all hatred — hatred and its decoy as one and the same — the unpardonable sin to be cast out and not healed. Then we must "gather ourselves up in God," in our own humility, our own peace, our own perfection and its infinity, rejoicing in the divine fact that hatred has never touched us or our affairs, has never done a thing, was never person, place or thing, and we and our universe have always been and always will be at the standpoint of perfection.

To the extent that we do this, we find and prove that God alone handles animal magnetism in His own way, in His own time; and we see immediate harmony manifested in our own universe. And for the sake of the so-called moral idiot — if we have not been doing this — we should begin doing it now. This sends the moral idiocy out of our affairs, one way or the other — more or less painfully, seemingly according to how long we have allowed it to go on in our affairs. This is the pure and final meaning of healing our friends. This is the real meaning of loving our neighbor.

The whole trick of animal magnetism today, then, is to make us think that healing others — especially those under the claim of moral idiocy — is to think about them. It would make us turn away from purifying our own sense of self and do something about someone else — help him, heal him, get rid of him. And if we see through moral idiocy and do not do this, it nags at us that we are neglectful, selfish, bigoted, isolationists, reactionary. Then it claims to work on a sense of personal integrity that it attaches to us, and uses as a tool to work on us, to bring us down from our pure sense of humility. Thinking about moral idiocy and reacting to it is not unselfishness. We are allowing ourselves to be mesmerized by moral idiocy. When we do so, animal magnetism has us doing exactly what it wanted in the first place, and we are now at its level seemingly doing just what the moral idiocy is doing.

We forget that maintaining our own true, spiritual, infinite selfhood is all we have to do, that this is all there is of our universe, our affairs, our friends. This is maintaining divine Science. This is Christian Science practice, seeing our own selfhood as one with God, and seeing our own selfhood everywhere, divinely embracing humanity and "none else besides." This is not saying here is good and there is evil, but it is humility recognizing suggestion, looking out from its allness and oneness, and from there casting out evil's hatred — not harboring it.

So let animal magnetism, with its claims of moral idiocy, be on the "hot seat" and get involved in its own turmoil. Let *it* feel the pressure, have the disgrace, frustration, failure. Let *it* fear, doubt, suffer. Let *it* be under obligation, bound, saddled, indebted, responsible, liable. Let *it* strain, struggle, sweat, kick against the pricks, go through fire and water. Let *it* be susceptible to mockery, misjudgement, misunderstanding, injustice, imposition, shame, scandal, revenge. Let *it* be disgusted, incensed, vexed, worried, irritated, enraged.

If we accept any part of this are we not moral idiots too? And we cannot afford to be, for it is up to us to maintain divine Science and see that it is not lost as it was in the early days of Christianity.

55

So let us refuse to think of ourselves or our loved ones, *or be thought of*, by friend, relative, employer, as personal sense. We must learn to cut ourselves off from personal thought. We express divine Science, the Christ-consciousness, divine idea. This does not absorb, but rather establishes our true identity and glory. Thus evil's hatred cannot fool, misuse, corrupt, or cast down.

Thus will we recognize animal magnetism, when it holds moral idiocy up in front of us, and refuse to let it make us tear ourselves down through a false sense of unselfishness, duty, obligation, resignation — duality — but will we rather cast it out. Our demonstrated health, wealth, radiance, peace, joy, through humility, is healing power and is all that is needed to convince our friends.

The claims of hate, malice, depraved will, cannot operate to use a belief of moral idiocy or the so-called moral idiot through perversion of the fact, to put its moral defilement, arguments, demoralization, moral blindness, corruption, deformed mentality, etc. as physical claims on us through this belief of perversion — the moral idiot believing he is all right and the spiritual idea all wrong. Thus we can refuse to be a medium for hatred aimed at the Christ.

Evil would work this way because it says that we are the sensitive ones and see all these claims of moral idiocy. They tend to be obnoxious to us, while the moral idiot claims to be oblivious and insensitive to them — not seeing them at all as claims. The belief is that the hardened sinner is the healthy sinner.

The fact is that the Christ-consciousness stands as a law of immunity to these claims. Governed by it, we will not take in these lies as real, nor be made to believe them, or to believe that we can do nothing about them; but we are standing as law, the law of God, to all so-called perversion or inversion, and we are turning the suggestions around and sending them back upon the moral idiot and the mental assassin from whence they came.

It is not so much what we believe about ourselves in encountering moral idiots, but what we believe about them that lets them in. If we believe these claims of moral idiocy when they appear to be associated with us, as relative, friend, neighbor, then we seem to take in their mental and moral sins as physical claims on our part, and then we claim to do the suffering, while the moral idiot goes blithely on, being a medium for the hate.

Therefore we can know that there is no such thing as moral idiocy or a moral idiot in all of God's universe. Right where the hatred and malice says it can use someone through this belief, right there man in his true divinity is unfolding and is putting the lie back on the antichrist, seeing its error, and causing the hatred to destroy itself. We can know that hatred cannot reach us or our universe, our work, our God-inspired purpose, through any claims of moral idiocy, to persecute, confuse, upset, demoralize, or rob us of our spiritual selfhood.

RADIATION AND ABSORPTION

(From *The Christian Science Journal,* April, 1887)

God, the source of all being — the atmosphere, so to speak, in which all live and move and have being — is radiation, continual action. Man, as His idea, possessing His qualities, also radiates His thought, comprising all that is good, harmonious, and perfect. That constant radiation of light is the armor of righteousness which always protects man from his enemy, the devil (mortal mind).

All mortal mind is the counterfeit, or opposite, of this Life-principle, and is absorption, blackness, and stagnation, which strive with apparent power, to set up its countercurrent of malice, envy, and selfishness, to render its victim an absorbent of all that is evil and erroneous, causing stagnation and death.

As man cannot at the same time radiate and absorb, by constantly sending forth thoughts of Love, Life, and Truth, whenever a delusion of their opposite presents itself, he may have a veritable armor against fears of weakness of every description, and so keep prepared for, and guard against, attacks from all directions. This idea will bear much contemplation, growing and amplifying with application. Thus — God, light, action, Life, Truth, and Love, is the invincible power, which repels and conquers animal magnetism, blackness, stagnation, death, error, and hate. Christian Scientists will find the effect of the approach and attack of mesmerism to be a sort of paralysis, or inaction of mind, which will be revealed upon the recovery of the right condition of thought by the vitality and Life that has conquered and destroyed the numbness and fear.

When such an attack seems to approach — by immediately reversing the condition of mind, and mentally inquiring of self,

"Am I radiating good, or am I absorbing evil?" — and putting that thought into action by addressing the counteracting thought of Spirit to whatever seems to be attacking you from mortal mind — you will set yourself free from bondage, and render yourself the medium of demonstration for those blessings you so freely receive from the source of all good.

For further information regarding Christian Science:
Write: The Bookmark
              Post Office Box 801143
              Santa Clarita, CA 91380
Call: 1-800-220-7767
Visit our website: www. thebookmark.com